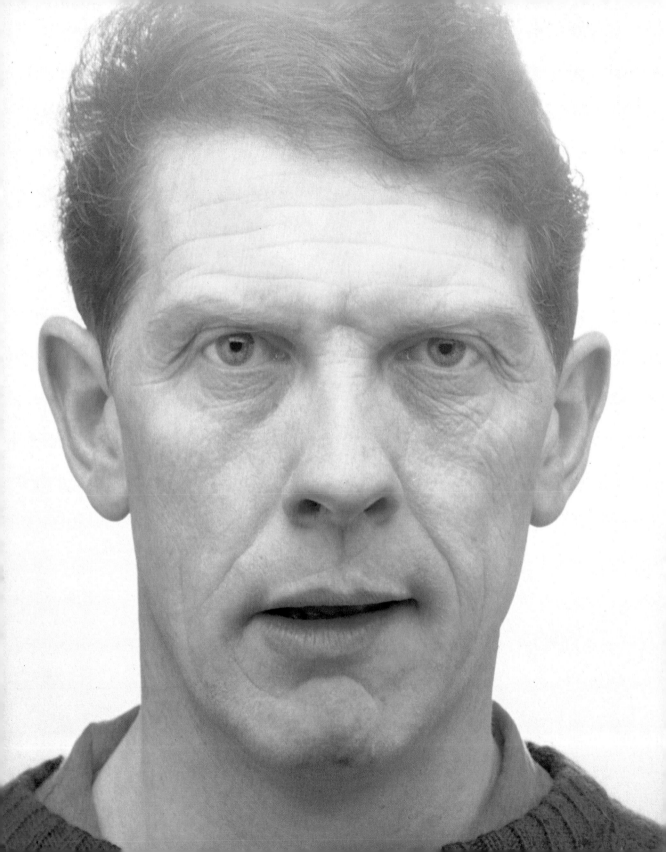

PHIL COOL

Cools Out

David and Charles

© Phil Cool 1987

First published Oct. 1987
Second impression Nov. 1987

British Library Cataloguing
in Publication Data
  Cool, Phil
  Cool's out.
  I. Title
  823'.91409  PR6053.0527/

  ISBN 0-7153-9131-3

Phototypeset by Chapterhouse,
Formby and printed in Great
Britain by Redwood Burn for
David & Charles Publishers
plc Brunel House Newton Abbot
Devon

Picture Credits:

p7 (BR) Pat Fleming
p18 D+M Plage/Survival Anglia
p11 (BR) Davies and Starr,
courtesy Amnesty
International
p21,95 (BR) Syndication
International
p44, 45 Milton Keynes
Development Corporation
p49 (BR) p95 (TL) Roger
Hammond
p55 (BR) Rex Features
p55 (TL/TL/TR/BL) Popperfoto
p64 Fish Trade Journal
p94 (BL) Metropolitan Police

## •FOREWORD•

**S**alve!

Observami longum itineram Phil Coolorum ad Numerus Unun in Britannia tunc ascendat Wythenshawe Labour Club. Sed multus fatuus walles exclamant, 'Get off, yer pillock!' et 'I've seen funnier weather forecasts!' Phil, frustrus et lacrimosus, dictat, 'O Wythenshawe! O misere! O all for decem quid cum non expenses!'

Ecce Phil hic hodie. Stellat in gigs ab Tyneside ad Falmouth, etiam selloutes bravo selloutque Royalty Theatre in Londinium. Multus popularis, multus autographes, multus 'EXCLUSIVE – COOL'S SECRET STRUGGLE' fabricius *Daily Mirror* est!

Et Phil Cool vanitas est?

Non. Invitates ad *Wogan*, etiam *Blankety Blank* et *What's My Line*. 'Nunquam,' dictat Phil. 'Ego humoristas, non Saturday Night dummy Monkhousianus! Sodit!'

Et tunc Phil scribavit livrum, *Cool's Out*. Spero est multus grandus chartbuster unum nolo secundum – Jeffrey Archer (quod minimus talentium!), Shirley Conran (frustra et frigidus quondam Safe Sex populus?) et periculosus, horribilus Wicked Willie books!

Si! *Cool's Out* erat librarum favoris Vaticanorum hic Yuletide!

*Infallibly Yours*

*His Holiness Pope John Paul*

# •FOREPLAY•

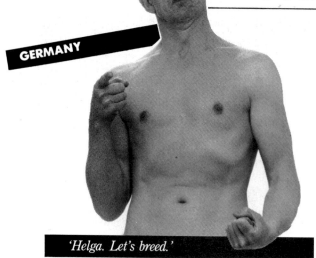

**GERMANY**

'Helga. Let's breed.'

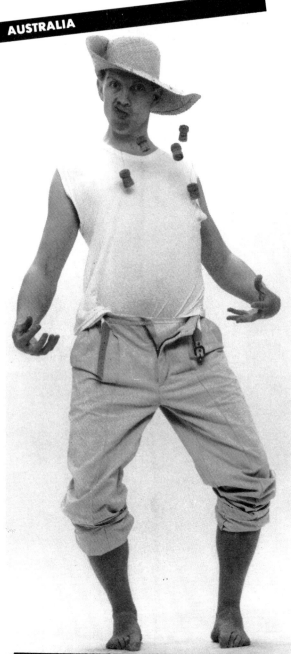

**AUSTRALIA**

'Brace yerself, Sheila – this is going to be the best seven seconds of your life.'

**JAPAN**

'Wayihitachisonysukimotowhenboatcomesinyo-
umeinbackofnissangetemoffyerbugga . . . '

'Ah, ma cherie! Amour de mon amour, clair de la lune, la rose de mon coeur, la plume de ma tante, le cointreau de mon clouseau, mon petit petit petit deux-chevaux avec des grands – but, ma leetle one, you are asleep. Never mind, allons-y . . .'

AMERICA

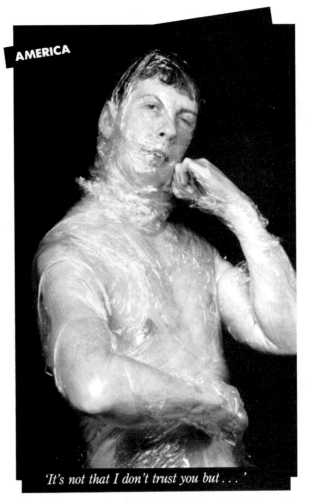

'It's not that I don't trust you but . . .'

ENGLAND

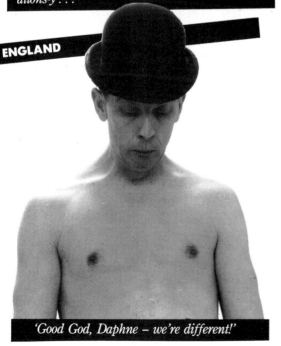

'Good God, Daphne – we're different!'

SOUTH AFRICA

We are unable to bring you further details owing to South Africa's reporting restrictions.

*Chat Show*

# MASTERCLASS

*with Terry Wogan*

Following the enormous success of BBC 2's previous Media Masterclass programmes *Game Show Crawling with Crowther, Laughing at Foreigners with Clive James, Looking like Princess Di with Selina Scott* and *Running Across a Field in Tight Jeans with Anneka Rice*, this Sunday sees the most revealing programme so far – *How to Earn £350,000 a Year and Give Your Ego an Outing Every Night with Terry Wogan*. In this exclusive preview, the man he calls 'the greatest Irishman of the century, possibly of all time' reveals some of the tricks of the trade . . .

'Hullo, it's old Tel here to explain to you, the common people, my public, some of the secrets of my astonishing international success. So, to get the ball rollin' let's, just for a laugh, pretend that like me you've got the basic requirements for a chat-show host: charm, looks, a lovely mellifluous sing-song accent, a good set of teeth, honest eyes, a sparkling ready wit, a brilliant, cutting intelligence, a thoroughly acceptable lifestyle and an agent who eats producers for breakfast. That's not bad for a start – but how d'you get your show above *The Antiques Road Show* in the old ratings? I'll not be telling you that because I've not yet managed it meself!

Continued

# OPENING THE SHOW

No one's interested in anybody but yourself so delay the moment when you have to share the limelight for as long as possible. Like this –

*'I suppose you're all wonderin' who me first guest is going to be. Well, whoever it is, he's going to have to wait . . . '*

*' . . . because old Tel likes standing here a couple of minutes, wibble-wobblin' his head around and going up and down on the tippy-toes . . . '*

*' . . . a quick shufti from side to side . . . '*

*' . . . and that little wry smile to the folks at home . . . '*

## CAMERA ANGLES

You'll be wanting lots and lots and lots of cameras in the studio. And this is how you should tell your producer to arrange them:

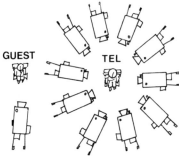

## BEFORE THE SHOW

After the old warm-up man has woken the studio audience up with one of them electric cattle prods they still use back in the old country, give the punters a bit of a thrill by making a brief, personal appearance in their midst. Talk to them for a few seconds – if you're in a good mood, let one or two of them touch your good self. Make them feel that teeny-weeny bit special, allow them to warm themselves in the glow of your charisma.

## THE INTERVIEW ITSELF

This bit's easy. Just allow your own natural charm to come across whenever possible. This sequence from one of my most legendarily successful shows reveals how it's done:

*Tel*: So Richard, now that you're a bit of a celebrity in your own right, I suppose you must get recognized sometimes.

*Richard Branson*: **Yes**, I do get recog-

*Tel*: So do I. Only yesterday, outside Harrods, signing autographs for four and a half hours I was. I just couldn't get away. (CONFIDING, AIN'T-LIFE-HARD SMILE TO CAMERA THREE) But, what with the recent success you've had, you go from strength to strength, don't you?

*Richard Branson*: Just plain hard work, Terry and –

*Tel*: I know what you mean, Richard (SIDEWAYS, WHAT-A-WALLY GLANCE AT CAMERA FOUR) In fact, I'm a bit of a grafter meself. Up at all hours I am, working meself to an early grave. And for what? A measly £350,000 a year.

*Richard Branson*: Could I just –

*Tel*: Thanks for coming on the show, Richard. It's been a pleasure listening to you.

## WINDING UP THE SHOW

It's been another triumph. I don't know how I do it, I really don't. Now all I need to do is make a couple of jokes about Dallas, plug me show for tomorrow night and, as the cameras zoom in for a loving last close-up of me old features, soak up the wild applause to the strains of me theme tune.

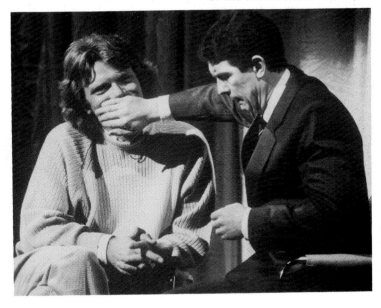

# FAIRLY TRUE STORIES

I WENT TO A VERY, VERY STRICT Roman Catholic school, where religious instruction took precedence over every other subject. So consequently, when you left the damned place, you were thicker than when you went in. It was an all boys school – I think the logic behind it being that was to get you used to a jail environment before you left. And as for the teachers . . .

One of them used to say things like, 'Right, where was you before now – you should've been 'ere yonks ago with them there books what I give you from 't last lesson.' And that was the English teacher.

Then there was a religion-crazed music teacher who would start each lesson by tuning up his violin, meticulously putting rosin on his bow – then thwatting everyone around the head with it, screaming, 'Right! Who went to Holy Communion this Sunday?'

All the hands shot up – except mine.

'Are you too lazy, boy?'

So I tried to inject a bit of humour into the situation. I said, 'No, it's just I like a bit of yeast in my bread, sir.'

Thwatt!

'Do you know what God is, boy?'

'Dog spelt backwards, sir?'

Thwatt! Thwatt!

'Insolence, boy (Thwatt!). Love thy (Thwatt!) neighbour as (Thwatt!) thyself.'

As for the headmaster, I'll never forget him. One day he saw me through his office window playing marbles, so he rushed out and took them all off me. Damn good player, he was.

No, they were hardly the happiest days of my life, my schooldays. In fact, I think I learnt most from the caretaker. He gave us marvellous science lessons in his boiler-house – all about how to extract alcohol from boot polish.

# The Lads' Prayer

**Arthur Shreddie-Hair here, lads – I want to talk . . .**

Our Father
Who art in stilled in the mind of
every true Trades Unionist
Hallowed Marx be Thy name
Thy commune come
Thy will be done in't West as it is
in-evitable
Give us fair pay, our daily red
And forgive us our best pickets
As we won't forgive that press bias
against us
Lead us not into temptation of
letting scabs off lightly.
But deliver us from Thatcherism
For thine is the commune
And the power, not the Tories
For ever and ever
Eh, men?

# PIZZAEROBICS

Thanks to the marvels of modern fast food techniques, a whole new form of aerobics exercise has been developed. Once it was thought that you gained weight if you ate pizzas but not any more – because what you *gain* in calories you *lose* in your efforts to get it down you . . .

# THE <u>ADS</u> THEY
# NEVER DARED SHOW

'Excuse me, miss. But have you just dropped a Wet One?'

'ANYWHERE,
ANY TIME,
ANY PLACE...

# SAFE SEX

## The LATEST news

The **Ministry of Health** has welcomed the growing popularity of so called 'hand-weddings'. 'More and more people are deciding not to marry in ignorance', a Ministry of Health official said yesterday. 'Your hand may be a bit grubby but at least you know where it's been'. Asked how he felt about his own right hand, the spokesman commented that they had been going steady for some time but that, at this moment of time, theirs remained something of an arm's length relationship.

# GOVERNMENT ACTS ON INDUSTRIAL ACCIDENTS

## SAFETY – The stars speak out

GRACE JONES says:

'If you must use helicopters don't forget to duck when you get out.'

**REMEMBER
WATCH THAT
CHOPPER!**

GOVERNMENT SAFETY COUNCIL

'Hullo, bastards. We all like a bit of fun but juggling with chainsaws can sometimes be dangerous. Remember to turn them off first!'
ADE EDMONDSON

author of How to be an

Incomplete Bastard

**REMEMBER
DON'T CHOP
THAT WHOPPER!**

GOVERNMENT SAFETY COUNCIL

# FAIRLY TRUE STORIES

**W**HEN I WAS A BOY, I had a dog – in fact, I shared the best days of my childhood with Rover. He was an enormous black, white and brown mongrel, a cross between a labrador and an airedale – with just a hint of Shetland pony thrown in. He was gigantic, with enormous paws. When he barked the trees and lamp-posts would bend . . .

I used to spend hours training Rover – training him to be disobedient – and he'd get up to all sorts of tricks, like nicking chickens. He'd wander off to a nearby farm, grab a hen, hotfoot it back to our place and drop the evidence on the lawn, from where this poor, dying hen would crawl under the hedge to wait for the last rites.

It wouldn't be long before the farmer was there having followed the trail of feathers. He'd lean on the gate and stare suspiciously at me and Rover as we sat innocently on the lawn.

'Where is it?' he'd say eventually. 'Where's that chicken your dog's just nicked?'

'He's never been near a chicken. He's been with me all day.'

'Then how come he's got feathers all round his mouth.'

'We-ell,' I said, as coolly as I could manage. 'We've been pillow-fighting, you see.' The farmer narrowed his eyes as I smiled like a little angel. 'He lost.'

\*     \*     \*

Years later, I thought, 'What a stupid name for a dog – Rover. He didn't look anything like a car.'

But then some people do give their pets really whacky names. I've got this mate who's got this dog with a leg missing. He's called it Tripod. His girlfriend takes it for a hobble in the park every day and she's completely unashamed about his name. No matter who's listening, she'll be shouting, 'Tripod! Tripod! Tri-pod! Here, Tripod . . .' And Tripod's usually fallen down a grid somewhere.

A lot of people name their pets in accordance to what they look like. I've got a cat called Kipper – it looks nothing like a smoked herring but it's asleep all the time. And this neighbour of mine has got a cat which, when you look at it from the back, has got this great curvy tail. He calls it Question Mark.

A few years ago, I had this lovely pet tortoise – I spent many an afternoon in the back garden with Dickhead.

'Hey, Dickhead,' I'd say. 'Come out of that rhubarb!'

That's when the next door neighbour used to lean over the fence with a handful of rhubarb in his hand.

'Talking to me are you?'

'No,' I'd say. 'I'm talking to my tortoise . . . dickhead.'

'What's your, y'know, your favourite, like your favourite bit of, like, comedy, Griff.'

'What, you mean apart from watching you do like straight roles on telly, Mel?'

'Yes yes, very droll, I'm sure. No I mean what d'you find like *really* funny?'

'Well, there's um, there's up that um Pete – '

'Whassat then, Griff?'

'Y'know, Pete 'n Dud – '

'What, like the Dagenham whas-names?'

'Yeah, that's right, that's right, that's right – the Dagenham whasnames and, er, that E.L. Wisty – '

'Yeah, great, E.L. Wisty, great . . . Who was 'e then?'

'Well, y'know, 'e was the one whose

act we like, y'know, borrowed.'

'What you mean, we like nicked this idea – '

'No, Mel, no no no no. Not nicked, *borrowed*. Anyway, it's not exactly the same, is it?'

'What, a couple of ignorant wallies talking to one another?'

'Well, *that's* the same o'course but – '

'So come on then, what's different?'

'What, you mean, apart from us not being quite as funny?'

'All right yeah yeah all right yeah – '

'Well . . . for a start . . . we leave these y'know . . . long . . . gaps, right?'

' . . . long gaps.'

'Yeah . . . long . . . gaps. Then we repeat ourselves to fill up the time, don't we?'

'Repeat ourselves?'

'Yeah, repeat ourselves.'

'How d'you mean we repeat our- selves?'

'I mean we repeat what the other person has just repeated, right.
It's called Comidé Verité – '

'Oh yeah – '

'Comidé Verité, that's what it's called – '

'What does that mean then, Comidé Verité?'

'It *means*, it means, well it *means*, we just keep on like this till we get to the end of the sketch.'

'That's easy then. Easy as makin' a few grand out of beer commercials, that is . . . '

'Right.'

'Right.'

'Right. Is that it then, Mel?'

'Yeah, let's sod off then, Griff.'

# MOTORWA

**N**ot only does he own a Morris Traveller but he looks like one. His back windows are full of green and yellow stickers announcing his recent membership of the Friendly Green Peaceful Save the Whale Earth Society. The

**S**ome time ago, I bought this Desmond Morris book, *Manwatching*. Now Desmond reckons that we all respond subconsciously to body language and that every moment of the day we're giving out these signals in the way we present ourselves to the world – without ever knowing it. But I was surprised that he never studied the area where body language is at its most direct – on the motorway.

If you get a chance, look at some of the primeval archetypes and throwbacks you find trapped on the average motorway . . .

In the slow lane you get the student rattling along at 50 mph . . .

**H**e's bound to be some sort of extremist because he's got a Ford Sierra – he's probably what they call an XR4-eyed rep. He goes flying down the fast lane, flashing his lights, blaring his horn – wally and machine in perfect harmony.

And Mr Mean is never happier than when there are

# WATCHING

thick fumes from his exhaust may well form a halo over the car.

Then, in the middle lane, lord of all he surveys from his cabin, is the driver of a gigantic juggernaut . . .

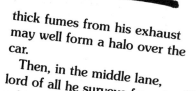

Yes, it's old Cholesterol-Brain. Driving eighty tons through the pouring rain at 70 miles an hour, creating a 250 foot wake behind and blocking everyone's vision, he's the kind of trucker who gives truckers a bad name. He has these vital statistics: 126 inch waist, 21 inch biceps, a 19 inch neck – and a two inch head. When he goes for a cup of tea in the rain he simply rolls a condom over it.

Then in the fast lane, terrorizing all the other drivers, is Mr Mean . . .

the inevitable road works holding up the motorway traffic. While the rest of us good citizens are moving over to the middle lane, Mr Mean has other ideas. You put your head out of the window to see what's going on – and you almost get it knocked off as he flies by at 90 mph.

'Ha ha ha ha ha – queue for ever, suckers!'

Then, as he gets near the cones, he slows up and puts his left indicator on. But all the cars queuing in the middle lane are so close to one another, you can hardly get a razor between them. Looking straight ahead, you can't help saying, ventriloquist-style, 'You're not getting in now, pal. No way.' Mr Mean tries a suave 'May I?' but there's no budging you, Mr Middle. And you're still saying through gritted teeth, 'Anyway, I can't let you in 'cos I've not seen you,' while pretending to look for something in the glove compartment.

Mr Mean's got nine inches to spare from the cones and he keeps edging in so that his left wing is almost touching your right one.

It's time for urgent action – and that's when being an impressionist comes in handy. Because now you can forget being Mr Middle of the Road, wind the window down and blast him with a Vyvyan broadside –

'Forgive me saying so, Mr Salesperson,' he says, 'but why don't you do the world a favour and have a nice head-on collision with a motorway bridge, you bastard!'

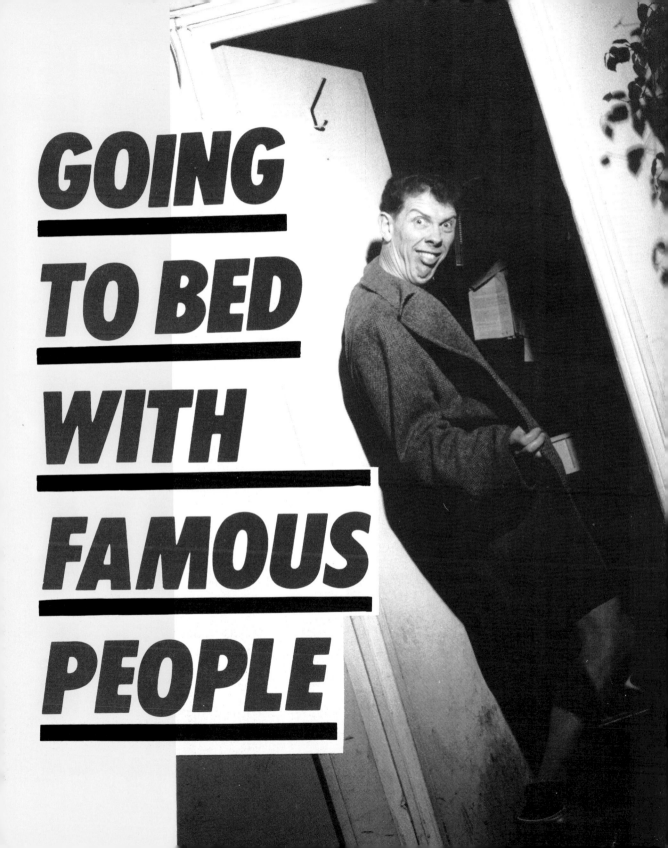

GOING
TO BED
WITH
FAMOUS
PEOPLE

**1**

**3**

**2**

**4**

**5**

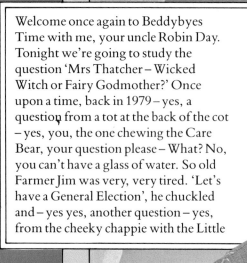

## SIR ROBIN DAY

Welcome once again to Beddybyes Time with me, your uncle Robin Day. Tonight we're going to study the question 'Mrs Thatcher – Wicked Witch or Fairy Godmother?' Once upon a time, back in 1979 – yes, a question from a tot at the back of the cot – yes, you, the one chewing the Care Bear, your question please – What? No, you can't have a glass of water. So old Farmer Jim was very, very tired. 'Let's have a General Election', he chuckled and – yes yes, another question – yes, from the cheeky chappie with the Little Pony who's peeling the wallpaper off – your question please . . . What? No you can't, you've only just been. Where was I? Oh yes, and the Old Thatcher won the election and kicked poor old Farmer Jim out of his house and nobody ever heard of him again. Then she made all her favourite broadcasters into knights and Sir Alastair and I have lived very happily ever after. Well, that's all we have time for – it's almost closing time – so it's a very goodnight, especially to you.

# ...some well-known fathers reveal

## MELVYN BRAGG

... the man was wild, untamed, with a bristling Northern manliness which the years spent as a brilliantly successful television star in London had failed to blunt. Women found his shy smile, his brooding, intense eyes, his oddly affecting adenoidal voice quite irresistible and there were times in his dressing-room, waiting to outshine another of his intellectual guests in front of the cameras, when he too felt pretty good about himself and longed to run his hands through his long, soft hair. Yet something was missing in the life of this brilliant, intensely attractive man. He had not yet written a bestseller. He would write a novel set in the tumultuous world of the Common Market. And, yes, he would call it *The Maid of the Butter Mountain*. And, yes, they would be interviewing him for a change. And, yes... Are you awake, children? It's just getting to the good bit.

# *their favourite bed-time stories*

## MICK JAGGER

Right, kids, well this is how it is, right? Way back in the beautiful, groovy days they called 'the sixties', newspapers used to print filthy smears like 'DIRTY JAGGER NEVER TAKES A BATH.' So one day I says to my communal girl-friend 'Come on, Marianne, finish your Mars Bar and let's get down to the Public Baths. I'll show 'em.' So she crawled out from under a Stone – you won't get that one, kids. You do? You filthy little devils – anyway off we go down to the Public Baths. And I'm sort of floating like on my back like, when all these kids start freakin' out. At first I thought it was because they recognised me, but Marianne told me to cool it – they thought I was a rubber dinghy. See ya then.

## SIR KEITH JOSEPH

Don't be frightened children. Uncle Keith's going to tell you a lovely story about when he was very very famous. It all happened when I was trying to banana skin the Trotskyite element in the Teacher's Flimflamwanglers' Union. Did I tell you about that? About when the ants crawled out of the exhaust pipe of my blunderbuss cuckoo clock? The reds are everywhere, you know. They're hiding in toilets. We've got to flush them – flush flush! Those elephants on the wall are pink – they're jumping, look – they're coming to get me, children. I hear the voices. Teachers, commies, pink elephants, they've found me. Help me, children. Phone No 10 and say Keith's doodlebugging. And keep those pink elephants away. Help! Margaret! Nurse!

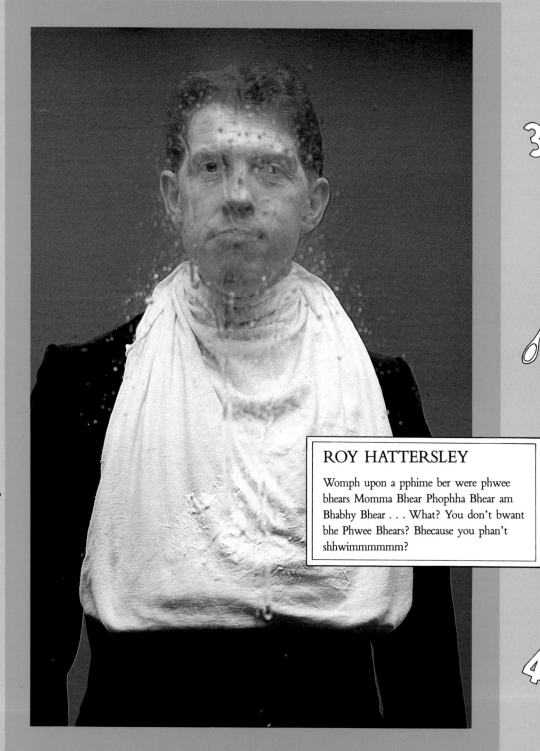

## ROY HATTERSLEY

Womph upon a pphime ber were phwee bhears Momma Bhear Phophha Bhear am Bhabhy Bhear . . . What? You don't bwant bhe Phwee Bhears? Bhecause you phan't shhwimmmmmm?

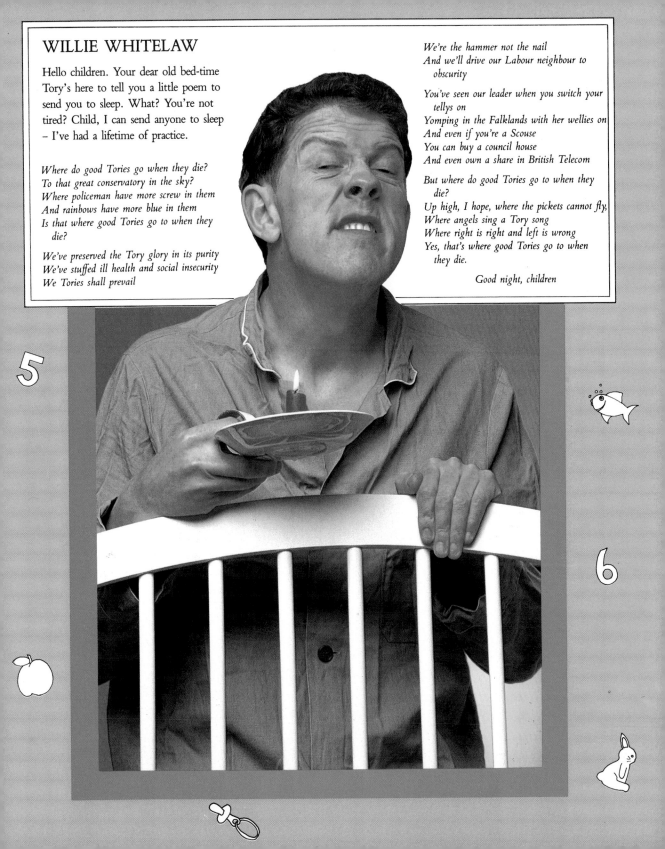

# WILLIE WHITELAW

Hello children. Your dear old bed-time Tory's here to tell you a little poem to send you to sleep. What? You're not tired? Child, I can send anyone to sleep – I've had a lifetime of practice.

*Where do good Tories go when they die?*
*To that great conservatory in the sky?*
*Where policeman have more screw in them*
*And rainbows have more blue in them*
*Is that where good Tories go to when they*
*    die?*

*We've preserved the Tory glory in its purity*
*We've stuffed ill health and social insecurity*
*We Tories shall prevail*

*We're the hammer not the nail*
*And we'll drive our Labour neighbour to*
*    obscurity*

*You've seen our leader when you switch your*
*    tellys on*
*Yomping in the Falklands with her wellies on*
*And even if you're a Scouse*
*You can buy a council house*
*And even own a share in British Telecom*

*But where do good Tories go to when they*
*    die?*
*Up high, I hope, where the pickets cannot fly,*
*Where angels sing a Tory song*
*Where right is right and left is wrong*
*Yes, that's where good Tories go to when*
*    they die.*

*Good night, children*

**O**ne of the greatest problems about being an impressionist is having somewhere to practise. I usually practise in my bathroom – it's the warmest room in the house, it's got a nice mirror, everything's handy. But the thing is you've got to do your impressions so I hate to imagine what my neighbour must think when he hears all these weird noises coming through the walls. One moment he's quietly minding his own business – the next, James Stewart's up to God-knows-what in the bathroom next door.

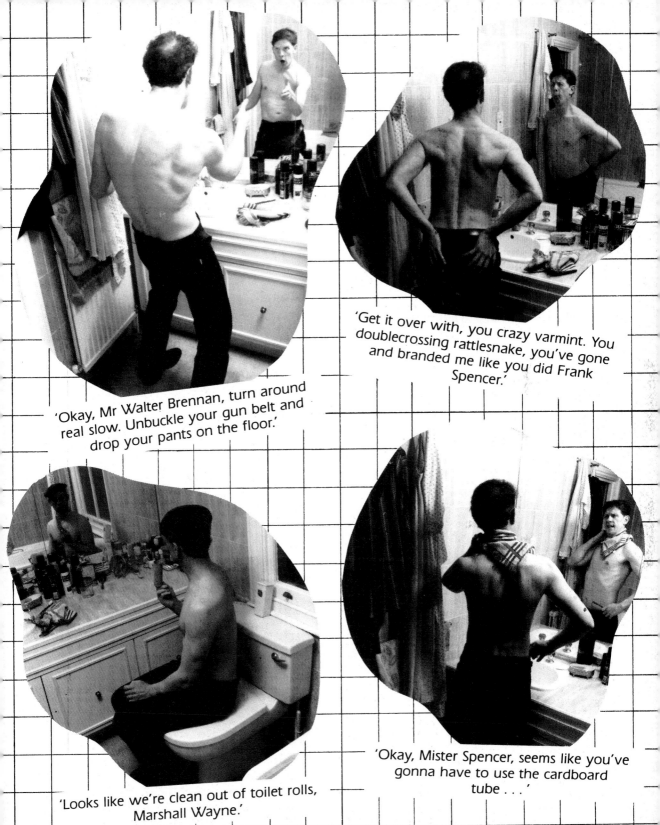

'Okay, Mr Walter Brennan, turn around real slow. Unbuckle your gun belt and drop your pants on the floor.'

'Get it over with, you crazy varmint. You doublecrossing rattlesnake, you've gone and branded me like you did Frank Spencer.'

'Looks like we're clean out of toilet rolls, Marshall Wayne.'

'Okay, Mister Spencer, seems like you've gonna have to use the cardboard tube . . .'

# FAIRLY TRUE STORIES

I WAS RUMMAGING IN MY PAPERS the other day when I came across a children's book by Bamber Gascoigne. Called *Why the Rope Went Tight*, it was all about a circus and, in particular, a clown. The reason I had the book in my possession dates to my one and only experience as a professional clown . . .

It all started with a call from a friend of mine from Granada Television, who at the time was working as Bamber Gascoigne's assistant. She told me that Bamber was launching a children's book the next day in a local bookshop and they were looking for a clown.

'All you need do is just sit there and amuse the kids,' she said. 'If we can't get you to look like the clown in the book, just say you're his brother and ad lib.'

Easy, eh? I agreed to do it. Which may have been a big mistake.

So I turn up at the book shop on the day in the baggy pants and funny coat I've been given and with a stuffed parrot on my shoulder, like the clown in the book. Bamber's already there, signing away, surrounded by kids.

'Oh look, children,' he says, sounding relieved. 'The clown has arrived – well interrupted – you can all go and meet him now.'

'Hello Bamber! Hello everybody!' I say in the Fozzy Bear voice I had decided to use and the kids rush over with their books to where I'm standing.

'You don't seem much of a clown to me,' goes one. The first sign of trouble.

'Oh yes I am,' I say, merry grin firmly in place.

'If you're a clown, why've you got ordinary shoes on?'

'Ho ho. Because I came out in a hurry.'

'Why are you talking in that stupid voice?'

Steady on, Phil. Keep smiling.

'Because it's the only one I've got, children.'

What was it W. C. Fields said? Never work with children or animals? And here I am working with children who *are* animals.

Just then one little charmer – Brian, his name was – looked up at me from knee level and, without the slightest warning, zapped me with a sharp uppercut just where clowns don't like to be zapped.

'Aarghhh! You little baaa – Bamber? Could you help me here, Bamber?'

'Well done clown,' says Bamber, still signing away as I hop around, doubled up in pain. 'Can you take it for two points? You're doing a great job. Right, fingers at the ready.'

And Brian's there – again.

'Aaarggghhh!'

It was uncanny – this was no wild lunge, it was deadly accurate. He must have been practising on some other poor clown.

I was just thinking to myself, 'If he does that again, he's going to get it with my stuffed parrot, the beak right in his head' – when he did.

'AAAARRGGGHHH!'

And, still in my Fozzy Bear voice – a true professional – I'm yelling, 'You little brat, come here and I'll 'kin kill you!'

I made a grab for him, he shouts 'Mum!' and all the kids scatter as their jovial clown lunges across the shop after his tormentor.

Brian's mother grabbed her little darling and bustled him out of the shop.

'Call yourself a clown!' she shouts over her shoulder. 'People like you should be locked up!'

And seeing my reflection in the glass door, I was inclined to agree with her.

# GREAT SONGWRITERS OF TODAY

*If it was nae for the accent*
*Ye might nae get a laugh*
*Because a Glasgae accent*
*Can really sound sae daft*
*And jokes about yer willie*
*Come out soundin' twice as silly*
*When they're aye delivered in an accent.*

*Nothing to condemn that's not condemned*
*Nothing you can tell to Orangemen*
*If you give war a chance, you'll get peace in the end*
*It's easy…*
*All you need is hate (All divided now)*
*All you need is hate (Everybody)*
*All you need is hate, mate*
*Hate is all you need.*

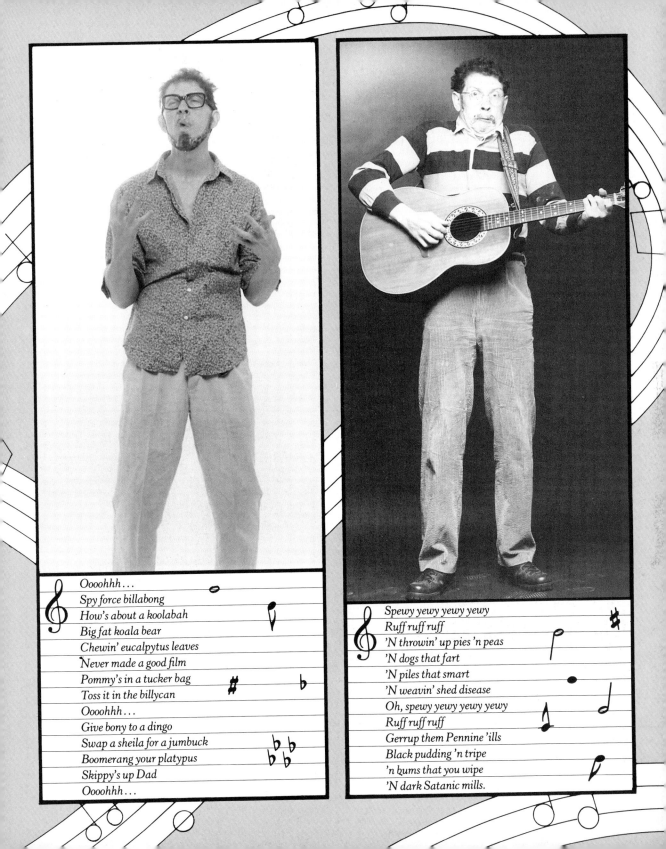

Oooohhh...
Spy force billabong
How's about a koolabah
Big fat koala bear
Chewin' eucalpytus leaves
Never made a good film
Pommy's in a tucker bag
Toss it in the billycan
Oooohhh...
Give bony to a dingo
Swap a sheila for a jumbuck
Boomerang your platypus
Skippy's up Dad
Oooohhh...

Spewy yewy yewy yewy
Ruff ruff ruff
'N throwin' up pies 'n peas
'N dogs that fart
'N piles that smart
'N weavin' shed disease
Oh, spewy yewy yewy yewy
Ruff ruff ruff
Gerrup them Pennine 'ills
Black pudding 'n tripe
'n bums that you wipe
'N dark Satanic mills.

# INCIDENT REPORT

**Name of Offender:** P Cool

**Address:** London Palladium
Oxford Street
London
W1

**Offence/Offences:** Driving without due care and attention . Driving with faulty headlight. Making porcine references to a member of the police force. Insulting a police officer by comparing him to a wooden dummy. Impersonating a wooden dummy to avoid arrest. Halitosis. Making jokes to a police officer in the course of his duties which the said police officer was unable to understand. Failing to respond to police officer's enquiries with the correct degree of cringing, crawling deference and respect.

**Statement:** 'I was driving home from a gig one night when I spot this young copper standing in a doorway. He's just finishing off a bag of pork scratchings - the nearest thing he'll ever get to cannibalism. Suddenly, he leaps out in front of my car and flags me down with a torch. It turns out he's a cockney lad who they've sent up north of Watford for a bit of hard training.

' "Ere,' he says. "you've only got one 'eadlight workin'. Can you not afford a motorbike or something? Only a dummy drives around with one light workin'. 'Ere - let's have a look at you." He pokes his head through the car window. "Ah well it all makes sense now, don't it. You are a dummy." He says with a mean smile on his face. "Do you realize you're a dummy, son? 'Cos that's what you are. A dummy."

What could I say? I just couldn't help myself. "A gummy?" I said, sounding like something that had just escaped from a ventriloquist's suitcase. "If you say I'm a gummy,

I suppose I must be a gummy. But I wasn't always a gummy - I used to be a policeman but I'm going straight now."

There was an odd choking noise from the policeman. "Cheer up constable," I said. "Have a swine gum." "Swine gum? I'll give you swine gum."

"Lets have a look at this 'orrible little mobile fungi factory you're driving."

So he shone his torch around the inside of the car, taking particular notice of the mascot hanging from my interior mirror - a little copper dangling from a noose. It's great when you go over bumps.

"Been drinkin' have we, son?" he says suddenly, sticking his face right into mine.

"Just a couple of shandies, officer," I say with some difficulty. Well, it's not easy talking and breathing in at the same time.

"You've 'ad more than a couple of shandies. Your eyes are swimming round like goldfish. But I'm not going to take you down town because I'm in a good mood, see? It's my birthday - I'm nineteen. I just wanted to warn you. D'you realize you're going down a one way street?"

"I were only going one way, pal."

"Pal? <u>Pal</u>? don't call me pal. What d'you think I am? A tin of dogmeat?"

"Sorry, chum."

That's when the police constable decided to bring me down to the station, after all. I can't understand the police treating me like that. They've no gratitude whatsoever. I mean, the number of times I've helped them with their enquiries."

*I agree that the above is a fairly true statement.*

*P. Cool*

There's so much depression knocking about these days. Well, I've just figured out what's causing it – it's the constant threat of nuclear war that's permanently hanging over us like a big black cloud. Now I've studied the film *The Day After* and *Threads* and anything else about nuclear war that I can find. And I've figured it out.

As soon as we get the four minute warning, I'm going to completely ignore the Government's stupid advice about going under the stairs with the cat and some sandbags and a tin of beans. I'll get it over quick – no lingering death for this lad. The moment the four minute warning goes, I'm going to strip off – and it's straight up the drainpipe. No under-

pants, nothing. Up on the roof, find the highest point, the chimney pot. Get on the chimney pot, starkers. Now, I live in Preston so I'll face Warrington I think. I reckon the Soviets will go for Warrington – it's a new development area. I mean, they're not going to bomb Liverpool – there's bugger all left there to bomb. So it's Warrington I'll face to get the full benefit of the blast.

But knowing my luck, it'll be a false alarm. I'll still be there the day after, with a big crowd gathering round in the street below.

'It's that Phil Cool,' they'll say. 'Him that does impressions on't telly. Come down, you pillock! Worst impression of a weathercock I've ever seen.'

# SPOT THE LOONY
# LEFTY COMPETITION

Can you spot the loony? First prize is a fun-filled day out in Wapping. Second prize is the same but without a return pass.

*Answer*
The one on your right is on his left.
The one on his left is to the right of left centre right.
The one in the middle is anybody's.

# TOTALLY UNEXPLAINED

**H**ardly a day goes by without, somewhere in the world, something utterly weird and unexplained happening – apparitions, sounds, spooky presences, visitors from other worlds, paranormal freakies of every kind. Now, for the first time, every instance of unexplained phenomena is being studied by a special government department set up five years ago by Sir Keith Joseph when he was Minister of Health and had just started seeing tarantulas in his Shredded Wheat. This highly secret group of experts known only as The British Organization for Noting Kinetic Events and Recording Spookies – B.O.N.K.E.R.S. for short – has recently been receiving information from around the world that has left members of the conventional scientific establishment quite literally wetting themselves with disbelief.

Here are just some of the weird events which they have been studying: So far, all of them are

# TOTALLY UNEXPLAINED...

# THE VINDALOO TRIANGLE

Ever since the Patel family established their famous Far Pavilions ('We do The Hottest Curries in Town!') Tandoori House in a sleepy side street of Acton, London, the area has become known by locals as 'the Vindaloo Triangle'. Because no less than *five* people have been seen to spontaneously combust as they emerge from the Patels' restaurant and attempt to light up a post-curry cigarette. Today all that remains of their *totally unexplained* disappearances are a few fragrant ashes in the gutters of Acton.

**The Vindaloo Triangle claims another victim.**

# THE HORRIBLE SLIMY GREEN CREATURE IN THE BATHROOM

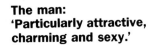

**The man:** 'Particularly attractive, charming and sexy.'

**The creature:** 'Horrible slimy green thing.'

A VAT inspector in the north of England was the subject of a *TOTALLY UNEXPLAINED* visitation from a creature from outer space. He was covering the town of Leyland, Lancashire and was visiting the house of an unnamed individual in the entertainment business to inspect his account books. The man's wife came to the door and called back into the house, 'It's the VAT man, Phil!' The next thing the inspector knew was that a horrible slimy green monster had appeared from the bathroom, sticking its tongue out and growling, 'We are *everywhere . . .* ' 'It was terrifying,' the VAT man recalls, 'I had seen pictures of this man and he seemed a particularly attractive, charming and sexy sort of person. I wonder if he knows a space creature is now co-habiting with his wife.'

## THE MIRACLE WORKER OF MACCLESFIELD

In a small council flat in Macclesfield there lives a little old woman who has mysterious, *totally unexplained* healing powers. 'I don't know how it works,' says Mrs Edith Small. 'Folks from the other flats bring their pets round here when they're feeling a bit poorly. I do what I call "a laying on of hands" – my hands get sort of warm when I place them on the pet – and that's it. The pet just gradually gets better, except in those cases when it's too far gone for my healing powers to work – then it dies.'

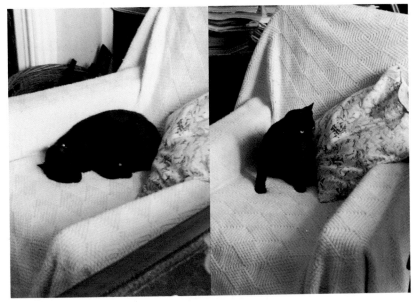

**Edith's healing powers –   before and after**

# THE VERY SENIOR POLICEMAN WHO HEARD VOICES

An unnamed Chief Constable of Greater Manchester was being driven to a meeting of the Responsible Society of Loud-Voiced, Big-Bottomed Women against Sex, Filth and Channel Four when he heard a voice, saying 'Calling all Chief Constables, calling all Chief Constables.' He told the driver to switch the intercom off, only to be told that the car was too old to have one – the voice was *TOTALLY UNEXPLAINED* . . . 'That's you, you bearded git,' the voice continued. 'And sit up when I speaketh to you!' Trembling and sitting bolt upright, the Chief Constable heard the following words . . .

'Thou shalt call a press conference. Thou shalt thunder mightily against the evils of the day – promiscuity, Sex with Paula, Eastenders. Thou shalt rabbit on until the world shalt say, Verily, this man has lost his marbles, he is as crazy as a bedbug.'

Stammering with fear, the Chief Constable asked The Voice why he had to do this. It replied, 'Because I haven't had a laugh for bloody ages – so get on with it, mush!'

And the Chief Constable has never been the same again.

**The unnamed Chief Constable of Greater Manchester**

# THE FLYING SNAILS OF ORLY

The folk of the sleepy French village of Orly, near Paris, have been startled in recent months by a daily shower – of snails. Asked about the phenomenon, staff at the nearby airport were unable to help, claiming that they, following the disastrous attempt to put snails on the menu of flights to Paris from New York, didn't even want to talk about them. To this day, the flying snails of Orly remain TOTALLY UNEXPLAINED.

**FACT:** There is no species of snail in the world that can fly.

# THE YODELLING YETI

Ace mountaineer Chris Bonington had spent months roaming the Himalayas alone in search of the legendary and mysterious creature known simply as the Yeti, or the Abominable Snowman. Previous expeditions had reported distant sightings of a large creature, footprints in the snow and some fairly impressive droppings but, until now, no one had encountered the monster face to face.

Bonington takes up the story.

'I was losing hope, to tell the truth – there I was, a grown man, stamping about in the snow looking for some ridiculous, mythical creature. But then, funnily enough on my fiftieth birthday, something *TOTALLY UNEXPLAINED* happened. I was just rounding a corner on a mountain track when, there it was, no more than five yards away from me – its coat was threadbare, it was breathing heavily and seemed to be having difficulty standing up. Then, to my astonishment, it started making a noise – in English! As far as I can remember, it said something like:

'Your 50th birthday will be a thriller
'Cos I am here, your pet gorilla
So good luck, Chris, as you do roam
Stuff this for a lark, I'm sodding off
   home!'

And with a weird, muffled curse, it shambled off down the mountain. I was never to see it again!'

**The Yeti – a photographic reconstruction**

# FAIRLY TRUE STORIES

Wythenshawe Labour Club. I knew I was on a loser as soon as I saw how I was being billed. 'PHIL TOOL'. It summed up the kind of mentality I was dealing with and, sure enough, I went down like a sack of maggots.

One of my early venues. The 'challenge' was to find the way out.

**I**CERTAINLY PLAYED SOME strange gigs in the early days. Folk clubs, for instance. Folk clubs to the 1960s are what herpes is to the 1980s – everywhere and spreading fast. And they were always full of plain-clothes morris dancers, fighting to get on stage to sing songs about dead sailors in Arran sweaters:

*My name is Captain Grant*
*And I am bound to saaaaayyy*
*I'm a-one of them bold heroes*
*Who ride the highwaaaaaayyy . . . '*

And then I'd get asked to private functions, like the Clitheroe Pigeon Fanciers Annual Dinner Dance. The place was full of pigeon fanciers, sat pigeon-toed, with a big basket of pigeons, in flat caps and smoking Woodbines, drooling over pigeon trophies. I'd come on and they'd all go, 'Look at that Cool-Cool Cool-Cool.'

You could often tell what the gig was going to be like by your billing outside the place. I once played a place called the

Then there was the horror of the night clubs. I remember one particular nightmare of a gig – it was called Quaffers. The DJ greeted me at the door and took me to my dressing-room through the club. So I'm walking through this dimly lit club and I look round – it's a huge, two thousand seater. Gulp.

But I follow the guy down a spiral staircase – down, down, deeper and deeper into the ground. At last we reach this basement and the DJ shows me into my dressing-room.

'Now the one thing you've got to remember,' he says, 'is this big wooden area here.' He pointed to a little wooden square in the basement. 'This is your rising stage. You'll know when you're on because it'll start coming up. You're on at eleven, so make sure you're on the rising stage then, ready and waiting.'

Later, I find out what's meant to happen. The DJ's up top in his pulpit and he presses a button. The motor starts. Brrrrmmm brrrmmmmm. You can feel the vibrations coming through your legs. Slowly the stage starts rising and the dance floor above starts opening up – one hundred thousand pounds worth of disco lights start flashing above you. Then – and this is the best bit the *Thunderbirds* theme starts playing at two hundred decibels. You are familiar with *Thunderbirds*, aren't you? I always thought it was a great series, although the acting was a bit wooden perhaps.

Anyway, I'm coming up slowly, the lights are flashing, the music's blasting out – dum de de dah, dum de de dah – and my head eventually starts appearing above the dance floor – dum de de dah . . . But the trouble was the drive belts must have been knackered because just then it started going down again – dum de de dah. Finally it makes it and as I appear slowly but surely, the music reaches a deafening pitch and the DJ goes, 'Ladies and Gentlemen, the man you've all been waiting for – the fabulous Phil Cool!'

I look around. There's twelve in – thirteen if you counted the coachdriver of this mystery tour from a hospice.

So I couldn't do my normal routine. But I'd seen this American comic on telly recently and I thought 'I'll be like him and deliver a stunning one-liner.'

'Hey hey hey,' I said. 'Flatulence will get you nowhere. Unless you're using it for fuel, that is!'

No reaction.

I pulled my little red diary from my pocket, slipped into my Eamonn Andrews and said, 'Come on out from under that mushroom because tonight, Ronnie Corbett, This is Your Life . . . '

Total silence.

I thought, what the hell am I going to do? So in desperation, I try something visual – my Aquaphibian. From *Stingray*. You must remember *Stingray* – even if you don't remember *Thunderbirds*, you must remember *Stingray*. Anyway the aquaphibians lived at the bottom of the sea – right scaly little buggers, they were. So I slip into my horrific Aquaphibian face.

Now sometimes I get this facial cramp – a total freeze of my features. Well, this occasion turned out to be sometimes. The bastard stuck. I pushed, I pulled it, I tried to explain – but no one takes an embarrassed Aquaphibian seriously.

Eventually the manager, who's almost having a heart attack by now, signals the DJ and, still groping wildly at my Aquaphibian face, I slowly disappear from view to the strains of *Thunderbirds*.

# EXCLUSIVE

# WHAT THE TABLOIDS SAY

A report on the year's press by our media correspondent Ten Bob Dylan Thomas Hardy.

The rent boy Watford worldly news of wrath, persecuteth thine fergie friend, outcast saved by the mirror pools of trivial truth. Exclusive hanky-spanky tale of sordid sinful sade, with Arabian night-hide under bedtime newsless worth to print. A hearty welcome is it not for those who russell gladly chat. A novel archers arrows pierce the bribe-maid goeth on holilay – low love two thousand smackeroo do take. George drugrisen twirling skirts defiant, laughing with the ginger virgin stubble clown upon the horsetooth empire. Dynasty of ignorance oh Collins of impulsive wedmock, where all Den's dirty do lust. Oh slant-eyed slip tongue dukedom embarrassed throne by wild outspoken trap. Out princess of green wellie fashion return not to sloane square one. Leave alone no one pretend so uncondemned, many paper sales of wapping money from barbed-wire-twisted facts inside the freedom prison press. Oh street of sunken fleet, oh thoughts replete with meat rancid filled, oh heat of –

(Thanks, Bob – you're fired. Ed.)

A lot of people believe that pets come to look like their masters but personally I can't see it — Geoffrey Howe doesn't look anything like Margaret Thatcher, does he?
On the other hand, a few of the entries in this year's Crufts did have a familiar look to them.

**Old Lord Willie, the faithful old bulldog**

**Barking Benn, the watchdog (pedigree destroyed)**

**Doctored Owen, the dalmatian that changed its spots**

**Kin-Kin, the Welsh Terrier**

**Elocked Bowels, breed unknown**

**The ancient Egyptians did it to Mummy. Roy Rogers did it to Trigger. Now let us do it to you . . .**

# GET STUFFED

Yes it's true. Thanks to the miracle of modern taxidermy, you'll now be able to be the same caring, generous, environmentally conscious person in death as you were in life. Because, after we've checked your wallet for donor cards and whipped out any internal organs which are in reasonable nick, we can help provide your nearest and dearest with that little something that will be missing after you've passed away – you! Instead of simply dumping your body in the ground or burning it to a crisp – a scandalous waste of precious human resources – our highly skilled technicians can replace the gunk left inside you with a unique filling fabric that will literally last for ever.

Imagine the pleasure a life-size, well-stuffed version of you will bring to future generations of your family in centuries to come. There'll be no more reading the family album for them – great great grandpa will be standing in the corner, looking as good (and maybe even better!) than he did when alive.

So don't hesitate to come in for a filling any time you're feeling under the weather. Our late chairman and his wife will be here to greet you – or, alternatively, if you want to see examples of the type of work we do, you can watch any episode of *Crossroads*.

*Choose from one of these functional,
decorative or educational poses:*

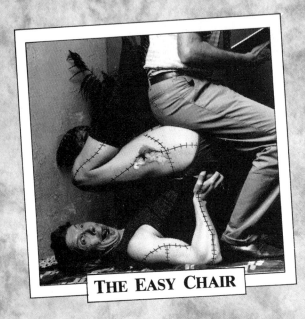

**THE EASY CHAIR**

**THE BIRD TABLE**

**THE HATRACK**

**THE WHERE-I'VE-ALWAYS WANTED-HIM**

**THE BICYCLE PARK**

**THE FAN**

**STUFF IT**

*We've got it all sewn up.*

# FAIRLY TRUE STORIES

I'VE HAD A FEW WEIRD JOBS IN my time – and one of the weirdest of the lot was when I got a phone call from my agent (I accepted the charge).

He said 'Phil you're going to Dhabi.'

'Oh great,' I said. 'Just up the road from Stoke-on-Trent.'

'Abu Dhabi! Be at Heathrow, Boxing Day, two o'clock.'

'Boxing Day! This was Christmas Eve and, to make things worse, my old guitar case just couldn't stand the trip on the plane cause it had been completely ruined at my last gig at a University May ball. The students had filled it up with beer – I wouldn't have minded but they'd drunk the damn stuff first.

'So I had to make a new one quick. I bought all the wood and the glue and the nuts and bolts and sponge and stuff, and you can take it from me if you're a novice at woodwork, the easiest way to make one is coffin-shaped. You can forget all the fancy curves, especially if the only tool you've got is a Stanley knife, with a knackered blade. So I started on this little coffin, on the kitchen working top, which was all pretty difficult really, cause at the time my wife was preparing the Christmas dinner. I ended up varnishing the wood with Bisto while she basted the turkey in Cuprinol.

Anyway Boxing Day arrives and I set off in the car, guitar case on the back seat. I've stopped at some traffic lights, when suddenly a motorbike cop appears alongside me. Hullo, I thought, Chips – a big one on each shoulder. He sat astride his bike looking at me – vroom vroom vroom. That was the sound of his brain ticking over. Vroom vroom vroom. He's thinking, bloody criminals – never around when you want one.

Suddenly he clocks the guitar case on the back seat. He bangs on the window. I wind it down. He says 'Where are you going with that little coffin?'

'Isn't it obvious? I'm a paedophile on my way to a Necrophiliacs' Convention.'

'I'm sorry, I do beg your pardon, sir. Allow me to escort you to the next junction.'

Eventually I get to Heathrow and make my way over to the ticket office. I'm humping this great box and getting some really strange looks. There's a fair few people waiting for tickets, so I plonked the box down at the end of the queue and sat on it.

I'd been sitting there a couple of minutes when airport security comes strolling up.

'Yours, is it?' he asks, looking suspiciously at the coffin. I couldn't resist going into my dummy routine.

'Not exactly, no – the ventriloquist has just gone for a cup of tea, and I've just come out for a bit of fresh air,' I said. 'But there again, you being airport security – you'd know all about dummies.'

'Move along, smartarse,' he snarled.

So, having got my tickets, I start moving over towards the check-in desk and then, of course, I had to run the gauntlet of ridicule from the maintenance lads. They're going:

He's getting buried in the morning,
Ding, dong, the bells are gonna chime,
Don't stick your nose in,
He's decomposin',
Get him to the church on time.'

Next thing you know I'm in Abu Dhabi airport. I'd really been looking forward to watching my guitar case come out of the luggage conveyor belt – it was going to be like a cremation in reverse – but I waited and waited and it never came out. Suddenly I spotted it – it was being carried away by four blokes, one on each corner and a group of moslem women in yashmaks. They were praying their little hearts out for the soul of the dear departed.

It was another twenty-four hours before I managed to get it back.

Starring Timothy Bottoms, Joy Bang, Rip Torn,

Christopher Plummer, Dick Van Dyke, Randy Newman,

Ava Gardner, Peter O'Toole, Steven Berkoff, Little and Large and Kate Bush

*Special guest star : Muffin the Mule*

**'Dick Van Dyke will bring tears to your eyes.'**
**Daily Mirror**

'Its dramatic climax left me feeling quite literally drained.'

*Daily News*

'I never really wanted to be a rock star. My dream was to be England's greatest cricket all-rounder...

MICK JAGGER

# RadioTimes

FRESH FISH

## Floyd on Fish

Returning next week – the man who put the fun back into cooking

**Hi there.** You probably recognize me. I'm one of the millions of folk who come over here to London every summer and enjoy your wonderful city, stand outside your wonderful Buckingham Palace in the hope of getting your wonderful Queen's autograph, or go down into those wonderful old antique things you call 'the underground' and get sworn at by your wonderful traditional cockneys as we stand on the wrong side of the escalator, and when we're trying to get from your wonderful Mayfair with its wonderful old whores on every corner to your wonderful Harrods, we manage after a couple of hours to find a wonderful old black taxi whose driver makes us feel at home by insulting us in those wonderful old Anglo-Saxon four-letter words before ripping us off by taking us the scenic route via the wonderful old suburbs of Plaistow, Ongar and Stoke Newington - you recognize us, huh? 'Cos we're still smiling at the end of it and, whatever you throw at us, we're still having a wonderful wonderful time.

**Now *you* thought we were American tourists. But you were wrong . . .**

We . . . are . . .

everywhere . . .

and we're . . .

having . . . a

wonderful . . .

time . . .

**T**HERE'S A NEW WORD THAT'S COME INTO fashion – 'speciesism'. Because these days, your average carniverous *homo sapiens* is very discriminatory towards his fellow creatures. For example, imagine how you'd react to the thought of a person with his head held in a clamp and his eyelids pinned back with crocodile clips while a big, fluffy bunny in a white coat dropped irritants in his eyes just to see what happened . . .

And we don't mean it when we say we're animal-lovers, do we? We mean that *certain* animals are okay with us, others not. So if you're a British ant, say, you're in for a pretty hard time because having six legs, a wobbly thorax and that old funky mandible isn't that attractive to humans. But if you're a dog, you'll usually be loved and cherished, and animal-lovers will be giving you chocolate drops and patting your head as they crush ants' legs, munch on chicken bone and try to pick the survivor of the Grand National carnage. Of course, we all know that man is dog's best friend . . .

. . . Unless the man happens to be a Korean. The Koreans like dogs in an entirely different way – they're part of the staple national diet. They sell dogs live in the market-place just like any other food. And unless you're a vegetarian, you can't knock them without being accused of speciesism.

So what if the roles were reversed? It's just another shopping expedition for the British housewife as she calls in on Mr Matthews, the butcher . . .

'Good morning, Matthews.'

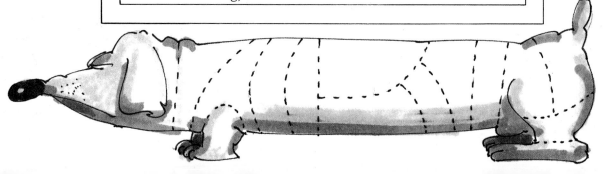

'Oh hello, Mrs McCreedy. What can I do for you?'

'Do me a couple of corgis, would you.'

'Ah! Very good choice, Mrs McCreedy – the Queen's favourite dish, corgis, and, oh, may I point out that we're trying to introduce lambs and hogs to the British dinner table. They're cheap and tasty too.'

'Ugh! Don't be disgusting, Matthews. I'm not having any of that!'

'They can't get enough of it over in Korea!'

'Lambs, indeed! I love those little, woolly darlings. And I couldn't eat a hog. My doctor says with my eyesight the way it is I might be needing a guide pig soon. Give me a couple of chihuahuas anyway – my husband likes a snack when he's on nights.'

'Right you are, Mrs McCreedy. And I suppose with Christmas being just round the corner, you'll be wanting to order your St Bernard.'

'Yes, put me down for a two hundred and seventy-five pounder.'

'Anything else?'

'What's your smoked beagle like today?'

'They're a bit tangy, Mrs McCreedy – it's all that nicotine from the totally justified laboratory tests, you see. But how's about a nice, juicy Doberman Pincher instead – they're boootiful!'

'How much is that one in the window?'

'What, the one with a waggly tail?'

'No, Matthews – the one hanging up by the scrotum.'

# *fisher of men*

## THE WORLD OF TOMORROW'S SPORT

# ROBSON FINDS HIS KILLER TOUCH

There was a distinct whiff of gunpowder at Old Trafford yesterday as Manchester United left their old rivals battered and wounded after a thrilling, full-blooded conflict.

The FA's decision to bring the crowds back to football by taking all restrictions off its big selling point, violence, has never been more decisively vindicated.

United had used their home advantage to its best effect by land-mining the pitch in a 4-2-4 formation before the game. As a result, Liverpool's left back was severely hampered by the loss of both legs in the opening minute.

But it was Robson who was the revelation of the match. At the end of the first half, he collected the ball in his own half and casually spraying the Liverpool defence with his fast-action automatic without losing control of the ball he found himself with only the goalkeeper between himself and glory.

Casually reaching inside his shorts for a hand-grenade, he delivered a beautiful lob that had the keeper sent off – in several directions at the same time.

'Frankly, we never knew what hit us,' the sole Liverpool survivor commented later from his hospital bed.

# HOLY PAGES

*A Cool Look at Religion*

**Featuring the most extraordinary literary sensation since The Big One hit the bookstalls almost two thousand years ago** — *The Secret Journals of Pope John Paul*

# VATICATICS

Memo - to myself - Second Coming

    Papers are still full of the Middle East conflict, now with the Superpowers getting involved. And yet Revelations say the Second Coming will also be in the Holy Land. What a problem!

    If the boss makes a surprise reappearance, be ready to revise hymn book. Like —

**T**WICE IN ROYAL DAVID'S CITY
**A**WAY AGAIN IN A MANGER
**A**S SHEPHERDS WATCHED THEIR WEST
    BANK ROCKET LAUNCHERS BY NIGHT
**T**HE SECOND NOWELL, THE ANGEL DID SAY
**O** REASONABLY LARGE TOURIST TRAP
    OF BETHLEHEM

Could do better, I'm sure - speak to an expert on lyrics. Norman St John Stevas???

## QUESTION TO CARDINAL HEENAN

Why did I get laughs during tour of Britain every time I said 'KISS my ring'?

Some **GOOD LINES** for future sermons

'Big? I'll say he was big. He was built like a brick confessional!'

'If that's true, I'll eat my inverted swimming costume!!!'

H₂O × $\dfrac{\text{LOVE}}{\text{CHARITY}}$ ÷ $\dfrac{\text{FAITH}}{£9500·00}$ = WINE
    SUBSCRIPTIONS

LOVE ONE ANOTHER METER

# CELIBACY GOLF

Remember to pray for —
Little Children
The Lonely and cast-down
The folks back home in Polska
Inter-Milan in European Cup
Ethiopia

Faulty Condoms? What is our line on this one?

## IDEA FOR A SERMON

'Dearly beloved, the Catholic Church — she is like a train. The cardinals are the guardsmen. The priests are the ticket-collectors. And you, my children — you are the passengers.

As the train thunders down the track through the tunnels and stations of life, we face the problems all the time. The work-to-rule of the unconverted. The leaves on the track of the Antichrist. And, of course, the Devil himself who will keep switching the points.

But, at the end of the day, I hope and pray we can hold our Bibles, the timetables, and say, 'Yes, we are getting there.' Good stuff!!! Or has it been used? (Check with Dave Allen)

Some smartypants asked me the other day about the 'Transmigration of Souls.' Had to give him a bit of flannel in Latin! Remember to check in Pope's Handbook what it means.

Issued by Cashin & Quick Ltd on behalf of Her Majesty's Government

# PRIVATIZATION NOTICE FOR THE CHURCH OF ENGLAND
## p l c

**THE CHIEF EXECUTIVE OFFICER ON EARTH, LORD RUNCIE**

In line with current government policy, the merchant bankers Cashin & Quick Ltd are pleased to announce the sale of shares in Britain's most prestigious public company, the Church of England plc. Now for the first time, ordinary members of the public can put their money into a concern that over the centuries has proved to be as solid as the legendary Rock of Ages Cleft for Thee.

## COMPANY HISTORY

Originally taken into public ownerhsip by Henry VIII, the Church of England plc showed steady growth over four and a half centuries of its existence until today it is the envy of every other Christian denomination. However a combination of management problems, left-wing Pinko bishops in particular, and a lack of a modern market image have led to a recent decline in its fortunes. With the support of a major advertising campaign, highlighting our unique '£100 will buy you a place in the heavenly choir' offer, the new privatized Church looks forward to the future with confidence.

## MANAGEMENT STRUCTURE

Our two-tiered management structure is divided into Management (Earthly Matters) and Management (Heavenly Matters). The Chief Executive Officer on earth, Lord Runcie, commented, 'Er, yes of course we in the Church must, er, be concerned about this because it's, er, the sort of thing we in the Church should – no, er, *must* – be concerned about.' The Chairman of Management (Heavenly Matters) has thus far declined to comment, although the general lack of fire and brimstone about the land is taken to be a favourable portent.

## HOW YOU CAN CASH IN

There are two types of shares available: Ordinary for the average churchgoer and the somewhat less valuable Guilt-Edged for those who only appear in Church half pissed at Christmastime and are getting a bit panicky about the After-Life.

**SO GET DOWN TO THE CHURCH ON TIME - AND DON'T FORGET YOUR CHEQUE-BOOK**

**WARNING: Multiple share applications are an offence. Penalties range from heavy fines to eternal fire and damnation.**

RELIGIOUS NEWS FROM AROUND THE WORLD

## Our Church Affairs Correspondent reports

### South America

There have been further sightings of flocks of nuns in unexplored areas of the Amazon basin as they travel through the jungle, loaded down with bibles and crucifixes, apparently determined to convert any happy, well-balanced, clean-living, dignified tribe of pagans they may find into a bunch of miserable, confused, sickly Westernized Christians.

Asked if they knew the nuns were approaching, a tribesman revealed that the first sign was usually a black-clad creature swinging through the trees like Tarzan, yodelling 'A-A-A-AVE Maria!'

### California

Following the revelation that Arlo 'Taxi Jim' Rattenheimer, who insists his disciples call him The

Master, was not, in fact, referring to poultry when advertising nationally for 'free range chicks', the famous sixties guru was yesterday being investigated by Los Angeles police. A spokesman for Rattenheimer stated that The Master was in a state of terminal freak-out with like the pigs invading his space when all he was doing was getting into a whole, totally unheavy God-is-love trip with a few of his young female disciples, man.

### Bournemouth

'Excuse me, are you a believer?'

Cosmo Smallpiece, Jehovah's witness area manager for the south coast, has reported another highly successful sales drive on behalf of Jehovah. His own figures revealed the following answers to his opening question on the doorstep, 'Excuse me, are you a believer?'

| | |
|---|---|
| 'Yes I am – go away, please.' | 20% |
| 'Yes I am – please come into my living room with your friend and talk about the Book of Deuteronomy for 6½ hours.' | 8% |
| 'Yes I am – why not step inside and join us in celebrating a Black Mass.' | 5% |
| 'Don't know' (Sometimes expressed as 'No', 'Leave us alone,' 'We vote Labour', 'Two pints please', 'Piss off' and other such ambiguous phrases. | 67% |

Mr Smallpiece added that a recent article in *All Along the Watchtower* revealing that AIDS was spread by blood transfusion had been well received by Jehovah's Witnesses. He particularly liked the way the piece was headlined 'WE TOLD YOU SO'.

# YOU TOO CAN START YOUR OWN RELIGION

Anyone can do it, you know. I've just started one myself – or revived it really. I nicked the idea from the ancient Greeks. They had gods for every occasion – war, love, thunder. But I can't be bothered with all those different names – Mars, Venus, Zeus and so on – so my god's multipurpose. He's called Kao.

Say it out loud to yourself. KAO. It's got a nice, godly ring to it, hasn't it? And the great thing is that Kao is the god of everything – hot water bottles, concrete garages, rip-top yogurt cartons, wrist watches.

So if you ever get a flat tyre, you pray to Kao, god of flat tyres. He'll help you through changing on the M6 hard shoulder.

(If there's no hard shoulder, you'd better start praying to Kao, god of recovery vehicles – and quick.)

Here is a typical Kaoist prayer.

'Oh Great Kao, god of pencil-sharpeners, why, O Kao, does this pencil lead keep snapping before a sharp point forms. I have already sacrificed ten HB pencils to you, O Wondrous Kao, at 12p a time.

Thank you for listening, O Great Kao, and goodnight.'

If that doesn't work, nothing will.

## RE-INCARNATION SOCIETY

CAN'T GO ON. THE LONELINESS,
THE HELL OF BEING ME. I JUST
CAN'T BEAR IT. FORGIVE ME FOR
WHAT I'VE DONE. IT'S ALL FOR
THE BEST. —
          GOODBYE
          TIM.

P.S. BACK SOON

# FACIAL KUNG FU

## THE ANCIENT ART OF FAN HI FICHA

In part of ancient China, violence of any kind was taboo, even in wartime. During this period, a new and entirely peaceful form of martial art, Fan Hi Ficha, was developed. Instead of slicing your enemy in half with one chop of the hand, practitioners of Fan Hi Ficha would scare the skirts off their sworn enemies by pulling grotesquely unpleasant faces. The art fell into disuse during the reign of the ancient emperor Ming who was so naturally ugly that every time he met another leader, war was declared.

In parts of the West where non-violence has been making a comeback, Fan Hi Ficha has become a popular form of peaceful self-defence. Some of the basic moves are relatively easy to perfect.

MITCHUMBUSHI

JAGGER LIP

HORGE MELHI

LAMBO

**BELLA MI**

**SAMHI DA VIS (JNR)**

**BUĠS BUNHI**

**UĠLI MUĠ MUĠ**

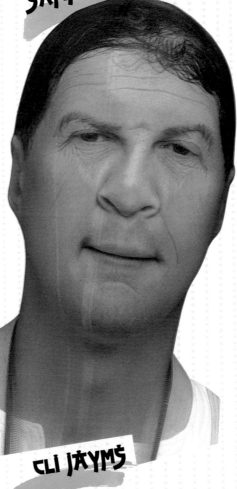

**CLI JAYMS**

**LEXI SALE**

# CLIFF says: LET'S CELIBATE!

*'Hey – celibacy,*
*It's the best policy*
*But if you can't control your emotions*
*At least take sensible precautions . . .*
**Your line, Freddie – '**

'Hey, listen everyone. I was just round at Una Stubbs' place, having a nice cup of coffee with my old friends Gareth Hunt and Ian Oggleatme – those has-beans (Get it?) – when we started talking about how it's always pop stars **against** something – first it was hunger, then it was drugs. "Gosh fellas," I said. "With all this AIDS and scarey stuff knocking around, there must be something megastars like us can do to help. So perhaps there's something we could do to help convince all the young kids to stop having, you know . . . S.E.C.K.S. and do something more constructive – like doing up an old bus and going on holiday. Strictly as good chums of couse." So, right there and then, me and Una settled down to write a rock anthem for the don't-die-of-ignorance generation – it's called **Let's Celibate** and you can find it on our new **Songs for Sensible Lovers** album – featuring some of our best superstar friends in the business.

So catch this – and you won't catch anything else.'

So Let's celibate
(Pay your health some attention)
Be your own best mate
(And you'll collect your pension)

'Yeah, stick to one partner
Forget promiscuity
If you want to win the human race
Invest in that packet of three...
**Tell 'em, Mick'**

'Ow, don't go sleepin' around
with strangers
Just 'cos your friends all think
it's cute
When you go to the chunky
dunky disco
Don't forget to wear a rubber suit...
**All together now – '**

♪ Just keep it straight
(Unlike some we could mention)
Let's be celibate ...

★ **Also available
on the**

Songs
for
Sensible
Lovers

**album:**

**Wherever I Lay my Cap**
Paul Young

**If I Said You Had a Beautiful Body
(Would you knock me unconscious)?**
Bellamy Brothers

**Alone Again (Healthily)**
Gilbert O'Sullivan

**Call Me Highly Responsible**
Frank Sinatra

**Touch Me
(With a bargepole)**
Samantha Fox

**Take a Walk on the Safe Side**
Lou Reed

**All You Need is a Cold Shower**
The Beatles

**Self-Abuse is a Many-Splendoured
Thing**
Matt Munro

**People Try to Put Us Down
('Cos we refuse to sleep around)**
The Who

**Johnny B. Goode**
Chuck Berry

**Help Me Fake It Through The Night**
Kris Kristofferson

**The Bright Elusive Butterfly of Totally
Platonic Conversational Non-Physical
Relationship**
Noel Harrison

**The Fool on the Pill**
Paul McCartney

**Sheathcliff**
Kate Bush

# FAIRLY TRUE STORIES

O OF COURSE, THESE days I'm used to all kinds of people coming backstage to my dressing-room after a gig – my wife sometimes, my manager, my manager's wife, some of the theatre staff – all kinds of people . . .

But one night, when I was playing the Royalty Theatre in London, I was visited by a real celebrity – Joan Collins.

After an exchange of mutual admiration ('I liked your show, Phil', 'And I like the taste of your shoes, Joan'), she asked me if I had ever thought of touring in America. I told her that I hadn't but that I was thinking of going out there soon.

'Oh, look me up when you come over,' says Joan. 'I'm just going back to do *Dynasty.*'

That was when I took my courage in both hands and came right out with it.

'You couldn't get me a part in *Dynasty,* could you Joan?'

'Of course,' she says. 'I'll ask the producer to write in a character with a Lancashire accent.'

I've been preparing for it ever since. In fact, I've already worked out my opening scene. Krystal and Blake have been fighting with Alexis. Just as things are getting really steamy, there's a knock at the door – and there I am, with a flat cap on my head, a couple of whippets and a basket of pigeons under my arm.

'Eeeeyup, Alexis, it's me. I'm your long lost cousin from across 't Atlantic in Wigan.'

What do you think? Will I get the part?

 I'M LUCKY TO BE ALIVE, ONLY recently I inadvertently wandered into a Hell's Angels' wedding reception. I couldn't help but laugh when I saw the wedding cake – black icing with studs around the top.

That's when the groom and the Worst Man started coming towards me, swinging motorbike chains over their heads.

I just couldn't help it, could I? I soiled my trousers right there and then.

They made me an honorary member on the spot.

EXCLUSIVE – **NEW GOVERNMENT MOVES TO CURB ALCOHOLISM**

**Anti-booze ad campaign planned**

HONEST • DECENT • AND • TRUTHFUL • AD • AGENCY

Cedric

I´ve been having thoughts about this anti-drink campaign the Government wants us to handle - can I run them past you?

First of all, we want a top director - the best English directors like Ridley Scott and Alan Parker have already done ads so why not get an American - like Sam Peckinpah, the maestro blood-and-gore director of _The Man Who Liked Killing Things_, _Bring Me The Fingernails of Alfredo Garcia_, _The Not Terribly Pleasant Bunch_ etc etc.

I´ve spoken to Sam and he´s hot to trot. He´s come up with a concept for peak hour TV advertising which could just get the punters choking on their beers. Here´s how it goes -

**FRAME 1**

JOHN WAYNE

'Weeeellll, I guess I've been on the trail now for nigh on four years. Weeeellll, I guess I miss all the comforts of home – '

**FRAME 2**

GRIFF RHYS JONES

'D'you mean Holsten Pils? Brewed so that most of the sugar turns into alcohol, eh, eh?'

**FRAME 3**

JOHN WAYNE AGAIN!

'No I don't, Griff Rhys-Goddamn-Jones. Trying to give me sclerosis of the liver, hugh? Who's yer sick-lookin' friend?'

**FRAME 4**

ORSON WELLES

'Carlsburg. Possibly the greatest lager in the woooorllld. So good that I feel it coming back up right no . . . now.'

## FRAME 5

BURT LANCASTER.

MORE JOHN WAYNE

'Hey there, Wyatt Earp. Whadda you think of these 'ere drunken bums clutterin' up our TV sets?'

## FRAME 7

'HE GOT ME!'

'OW!'

'I'M DEAD!'

## FRAME 6

'These goddamn alkies are goddamn everywhere, Marshall. Let's stop them peddlin' their filthy liquour round here for good and all . . . '

## FRAME 8

YOU KNOW WHO

'I guess they won't be drinkin' no Carling Goddamn Black Label . . . '

*'I was a bit surprised when the officer interviewing me asked me how I looked in a cocktail dress...'*

*CAPTAIN NICK SMYTH*

# A

S NICK SMYTH discovered, there's more to the modern army than marching about, shouting at each other and getting yourself all muddy. Because the modern army officer needs to be as groovy and fashion-conscious as the next chap.

For instance, here are some of the glorious creations they'll be wearing on manoeuvres this season.

**Blending nicely into the background, Gareth Rambo-Smith is wearing this absolutely darling little hollow tree number, enhanced by a subtle gorse twig motif. The turf hat is by Percy Thrower, make-up by Cow Pat. Gorgeous, isn't he?**

Here's Brian 'the Darling of Dartmoor' Hoskins in a stunning little number he designed himself. You can creep up on me any time, Brian, but if you don't cover those lily-white buttocks when you're retreating, you're going to get your bloody brains blown out, aren't you, you 'orrible little man you.

A few years in today's modern army and you'll be fit for any job that Civvy Street can offer – mercenary, male stripper or, if you're really macho, a presenter on Blue Peter. So why don't you call us some time – we'd just love to meet you.

# PRINCE EDWARD'S SERGEANT-MAJOR SPEAKS OUT

**Left right left right left right left right – on the double, you 'orrible** little Prince – atten-SHUN! Cann yourself a man, do you? your royal highness? Do you realize that £18,000 of tax-payers' money has been spent hitherto so far to this point in time on your training. STOP CRYING WHEN I'M TALKING TO YOU! Here, use my hanky, Your Highness, have a good blow, there's a good lad. Better. £18,000! To train a mollycoddled little Cambridge wimp like you to become one of us Lympstone livin' legends – and now Mr Taxpayer is going to pay out *another* £9,000 to buy you out. And why? No, Your Highness, not because the lady loves Milk Tray.

But because little Eddy-Weddy has changed his bleedin' little royal mind, you – wait for it – BASTARD! Metaphorically speaking of course your royal highness, no reflection on His Royal Worship your father. Now there's a man for you. Hard as nails, he is. Came on a survival course with us once – and he survived. Stop shiverin', you 'orrible little excuse for an Action Man. So 'ow much you cost the taxpayer then? Let me see now – £18,000 plus £9,000. That's . . . that's . . . £24,000 wasted! Think of the Space Invader we could 'ave got for the marines for that sort of money, not to mention the porno mags and marijuana. One more thing before I

dismiss you, you snivellin' little worm. WAIT FOR IT!!!! Could I have your autograph your Royal Highness, sir? It's not for me, sir, it's the wife. That you kindly. Now get out of my sight! Left right left right left right give me love to your Mum left right left right good luck with the theatre left right left right left right left right left . . .

# CLASSIFIED

Phil Cool and David & Charles Ltd are grateful to the following manufacturers for their help in financing this book.

## Don't gob all over the place!

Do you have a nasty catarrh problem? Not any more! This superbly designed mucous collector can save you embarrassment on every occasion.

**MUCATCH**

**Don't leave home without it**

£4.99

---

## GIVE THAT CAR BURGLAR A SHOCK HE WON'T FORGET

The
Mr Spikey Alarm

(Tested in police stations across the country)                    £9.95

---

## BACKACHE?

You will have when you try and sit in our unique DISCSLIPPER CHAIR™. It has no less than 198 positions, not one of them comfortable.
£59.95

---

## THE FUCKOO CLOCK

Startle your friends with the revolutionary timepiece that Mary Whitehouse wants to ban! It tells the time and abuses you at the same time!

Standard model      £19.99
Spitting model      £35.00

---

## ATTENTION, ALL RANDY BASTARDS!

The Up All Night Reusable Condom is now available in all good sex shops . . .

'With this one special protective from Up All Night, I can get through all these . . .'

£3.99 for a packet of one

# ADVERTISEMENTS

# GREAT SMOKER'S EXCUSES

I suppose every occupation has its hazards. My occupational hazard over the years has been smoking – passive smoking. Breathing in secondhand cigarette fumes in night clubs. I wish people would stop, I really do. Just because they've decided to turn their own lungs into a couple of kippers I've got to have mine cured as well. But just try asking people to stop and listen to the excuses they come up with . . .

'Let's face it, if it wasn't for the money we smokers pay in tax every year, the country would be bankrupt.'

'If I stopped, I wouldn't know what to do with my hands.'

'You can offer them round and make lots of friends!'

Walk down any street and you inhale more poison from car exhaust than you do if you smoke sixty a day . . .'

'My doctor says it's okay if I stick to the same brand.'

'A cigarette has that certain . . .'

'Give up smoking? It's the only pleasure I've got left in life.'

# PHIL COOL – AN ARTIST FOR ~~ALL~~ *CLOSING* TIME

An appreciation by
his close friend
Melvyn Bragg

The South Crank Show has
always been dedicated to bringing in-depth
documentaries concerning the lives and
works of the greatest of our abstract,
unusual, alternative artists of all kinds to
the attention of the intellectual viewer.

Tonight we look at the quite awe-
inspiring life of Phil Cool and pose the
question: Just what kind of artist can con-
sume so much alcohol and yet still live a life
of feverish creative activity in the snow-
covered hills of his native Lancashire?

He leaves us, for example, this
astonishing masterpiece.

Like so much of Cool's more
spontaneous work this one 'Where's
the 'kin window?', was created after a
Chinese Special Chop Suey on top of
seventeen pints of Guinness – the
Guinness which we find so often lies at the
very centre of his work.

Yet the delicate regurgitated pastels,
simply and evenly balanced, of that masterpiece pales into insignificance beside the
work he left so copiously in this very tele-
phone box almost every night after being

thrown out of the public bar of his beloved Black Horse.

A complete and, as so many people discovered to their cost, unavoidable expression of Cool's essence, 'Where's the 'kin toilet?' works its magic both on the eye and the nose of the observer.

If Van Gogh was famous for his passion for the colour yellow, then green was Cool's forte. Green was to be found everywhere in his life – it was the colour of his skin, his eyes, his underpants and, on one occasion when it produced the famous 'You're going to 'kin regret this, ossifer', an absolute masterpiece in crystals.

Yet the colour red also played a part in Cool's varied and unpredictable artistic life. After paying his daily homage to the memory of the man who helped influence so much of his work, Johnnie Walker, his dramatic and radical redesign of this glass door reveals a generous outpouring of this red motif.

Sadly, 'Who shut the 'kin door?' was to be one of his last works. During a lengthy tour of Germany, researching into the artistic potential of the bierkeller, he expressed his deep compulsion to impose that famous Bruegelesque version of anarchy on the smooth contours of his own car, while making his way home on the autobahn.

This tour de force, posthumously entitled 'Why's everyone driving on the wrong 'kin side of the road?' seems likely to remain his best known work.

We shall not see his like again.

Editor: Terence Blacker
Art Director: Roger Hammond
Design: Grub Street Design, London
Original Photographs: Mike Henton
Illustrations: Russell Jones

Well, I think everyone involved in this project
deserves a big pat on the – the – the

Oh dear, I seem to have done it again . . .